Scottish, Irish & Welsh Verses
Edited by Claire Tupholme

First published in Great Britain in 2007 by:
Young Writers
Remus House
Coltsfoot Drive
Peterborough
PE2 9JX
Telephone: 01733 890066
Website: www.youngwriters.co.uk

All Rights Reserved

© *Copyright Contributors 2006*

SB ISBN 1 84602 723 3

Foreword

Young Writers was established in 1991 and has been passionately devoted to the promotion of reading and writing in children and young adults ever since. The quest continues today. Young Writers remains as committed to the nurturing of poetic and literary talent as ever.

This year's Young Writers competition has proven as vibrant and dynamic as ever and we are delighted to present a showcase of the best poetry from across the UK and in some cases overseas. Each poem has been selected from a wealth of *A Pocketful Of Rhyme* entries before ultimately being published in this, our fourteenth primary school poetry series.

Once again, we have been supremely impressed by the overall quality of the entries we have received. The imagination, energy and creativity which has gone into each young writer's entry made choosing the poems a challenging and often difficult but ultimately hugely rewarding task - the general high standard of the work submitted ensured this opportunity to bring their poetry to a larger appreciative audience.

We sincerely hope you are pleased with this final collection and that you will enjoy *A Pocketful Of Rhyme Scottish, Irish & Welsh Verses* for many years to come.

Contents

Ballee Primary School, Ballymena

Curtis Penny (10)	1
Danielle Campbell (11)	2
Chelsea Mark (10)	3
Benjamin Campbell (11)	4
Megan Stewart (10)	5
Geoffrey Dunlop (10)	6
James Douglas (10)	7
Rebecca Hempsey (10)	8
Paul Bell (10)	9
Daniel Bainbridge (10)	10
Joseph Nixon (10)	11
Carson Boyd (10)	12
Naomi Doherty (10)	13

Enniskillen Model Primary School, Enniskillen

Jack Thompson (9)	14
Emma Nixon (9)	15
Luke Todd (9)	16
Mark Haskins (10)	17
Harry McCurry (9)	18
James Abraham (9)	19
Caroline Murphy (9)	20
Emma Shaw (9)	21
Adam Carson (9)	22
Courteney Moore (9)	23
Aaron Coalter (9)	24
Sophie Jordan (9)	25
Judith Cathcart (9)	26

Fair Isle Primary School, Shetland

Erin Welch (11)	27
Melissa Welch (7)	28
Amy Stout (11)	29
Oliver Harrison (9)	30

Lourdes Primary School, Carrickfergus

Sean Austin (8)	31

Victoria McKendrick (8)	32
Luke Herdman (9)	33
Peter Shannon (8)	34
Olivia Lennox (9)	35
Matthew Murray (11)	36
Bronagh Stewart (11)	37
Katie McKendrick (10)	38
Matthew Maguire (10)	39
Pierce Woods (9)	40
Ciara McCabe (10)	41
David Glanville Reid (10)	42

Mill O'Forest Primary School, Stonehaven

Katie Gordon (11)	43
Angus Matheson (11)	44
Kieran Johnson (11)	45
Rachael Craig (11)	46
Victoria Paisley (11)	47
Lee Ramage (11)	48
Michael Blacklaw (11)	49
Caitlin Milne (11)	50
Sam Jones-Lawman (11)	51
Stuart Moir (10)	52
Rebecca Yvonne Watt (11)	53
Shannon Smith (11)	54
Kimberly Dickie (11)	55
Kirsty Thomson (11)	56
Ryan Campbell (11)	57
Jason Kelly (10)	58
Jonathan Penman (11)	59
Rebecca Turner (8)	60
Bethany Nicol (9)	61
Amy Robertson (9)	62
Chelsea Lobban (9)	63
Beth Johnson (9)	64
Anna Jenneson (9)	65
Jack Neill (8)	66
Mark Leith (9)	67
Lauren Smlth (9)	68
Tegan Wilson (9)	69
Cameron Pyper (9)	70

Lyndsay Clark (10)	71
Jemma Campbell (9)	72
Ashleigh Mackay (9)	73
Jodie Kirk (9)	74
Paige Howey (8)	75
Nicole Johnston (11)	76
Michael Dunlop (11)	77
Kelsey Stewart (9)	78
Amy Gillies (9)	79
Alana Nicol (10)	80
Emma Hunter (9)	81
Robert Barry Cruickshank (9)	82
Liam Ferries (10)	83
Rebekah Laing (9)	84
Cara Findlay (10)	85
Roddyne Mentiplay (9)	86
Stephanie Mair (10)	87
Brodie Cummins (9)	88
Catherine Ritchie (9)	89
Tonicha Masson (10)	90
Connor Douglas (10)	91
Kim Mellis (11)	92
Sean Leith (10)	93
Jack Spence (11)	94
Heather Gerrard (9)	95
Serena Masson (9)	96
Katie Cruickshank (8)	97
Megan Robertson (9)	98
Jade Reeveley (9)	99
Heather Dryburgh (8)	100
Elliot Johnson (8)	101
Hannah Mackenzie (10)	102
Jennifer Ogg (11)	103
Sophie Christie (11)	104
Finlay Milne (11)	105
Emma Gordon (11)	106
Grant Begg (11)	107
Becca Stewart (11)	108
Sarah-Louise Milne (11)	109
Craig Forbes (11)	110
Hannah Duncan (10)	111
Rachel Eastcroft (11)	112

Ryan Brown (10)	113
Kerry Campbell (10)	114
Karris Knowles (10)	115
Fiona Craigen (10)	116
Douglas Blacklaw (10)	117
Megan McMillan (10)	118
India Henderson (9)	119
Lucia Arandia (10)	120
Jordan Henderson (10)	121
Jordan Butchart (10)	122

Nant Y Parc Primary School, Senghenydd

Cerys James (7)	123
Ella Day (7)	124
Sophie Birkinshaw (7)	125
Nadine Thomas (8)	126
Izaak Wallen (7)	127
Lewis Thomas (7)	128
James Ritchings (7)	129
Gethin Pearce (9)	130
Tim Crothers (9)	131
Aliesha Crowley	132
Jack Cossins (9)	133

Pittencrieff Primary School, Dunfermline

Daniel Banister (10)	134
Shaun Cuthbert (10)	135
Marie Sarah Philbin (10)	136
Jenny Milne (10)	137
Mairi Munro (10)	138
Matthew Koch (10)	139
Michael Waterworth (10)	140
Ross Atherton (9)	141
Mark Avery (9)	142
Afton Ritchie (9)	143
Bethoch McLeman (10)	144
Rhea Patel-McCrossan (10)	145
Paige Summerson (9)	146
Jade McCathie (10)	147
Morgan Steedman (10)	148
Daniel Halpin (10)	149

Eve Mossman (9) — 150
Dina Campbell (9) — 151

Victoria Primary School, Carrickfergus
Karl McClean (10) — 152
David Robert Algeo Douglas (10) — 153
Courtney Gibb (9) — 154
Judith Louise Scott (9) — 155
Jamie Lee Livingston (9) — 156
Nicola Jayne Curran (9) — 157
Danielle Lesley Brush (9) — 158
Naomi Hannah Watson (10) — 159
Rory Aron Magill (9) — 160
Ellen Crawford (9) — 161
Rebekah Kirkpatrick (9) — 162
Matthew Hogg (9) — 163
Rebecca Anderson (10) — 164
Gemma McArthur (9) — 165
Erin McKeown (10) — 166
Jason Kennedy (10) — 167
Marc William Templeton (9) — 168
Clara Eve Montgomery (9) — 169
Andy Wilson (9) — 170
Rebecca McCausland (9) — 171
Shannon Laughlin (10) — 172
Kennedy Herron (9) — 173
Matthew Larkham (9) — 174
Aimee Patterson (9) — 175
Chloe Park (9) — 176
Connie Mary Yvonne Blair (9) — 177
Loni-Ann Steenson (10) — 178
Katherine McKinley (10) — 179
Paul Nelson (10) — 180
Jordan McCully (10) — 181
Katie Ann Houston (9) — 182
Joshua Daly (9) — 183
Cara Leathem (9) — 184
Alex Steenson (9) — 185
Lucy Hannah Sempey (9) — 186

The Poems

Happiness

It looks like daffodils in spring
It sounds like birds chirping when the sun comes up
It tastes like a Dairy Caramel melting in my mouth
It feels like a yellow pastel rubbing in my fingers
It reminds me of the sun rising up in the morning
It smells like orange juice and bacon.

Curtis Penny (10)
Ballee Primary School, Ballymena

Happiness

Happiness sounds like a song of a bird singing in a tree
It tastes like a river gulping down my throat
It smells like fresh air flowing in my nose
It looks like the beautiful sun shimmering in the snowy blue sky
It feels like a warm, soft puppy lying beside the fire
It reminds me of how I felt when I brought my puppy in
From the cold winter's day.

Danielle Campbell (11)
Ballee Primary School, Ballymena

Love

Love is red like a big, juicy strawberry waiting to be picked
It sounds like birds singing
It tastes like grapes
It smells like fresh flowers
It looks like a heart
It feels like a soft kitten
It reminds me of happiness.

Chelsea Mark (10)
Ballee Primary School, Ballymena

Anger

Anger is red like a burning fire exploding in the sun
Anger sounds like fireworks in the deep, dark sky
Anger tastes like a red drink boiling on the stove
Anger looks like Rooney exploding on the football pitch
Anger feels like a rock hitting you so hard it bruises you
Anger reminds me of a fearless dog with red eyes.

Benjamin Campbell (11)
Ballee Primary School, Ballymena

Love

Love is like a red rose shimmering in the sweet spring air
It sounds like seagulls singing happily on the beach
It tastes like chocolate melting in the burning sun
It smells like cheery, fresh flowers ready to be picked
It looks like newborn tiger cubs playing calmly in the moonlight
It feels like a horse's hair ready to be groomed
It reminds me of pink silk running down my skin.

Megan Stewart (10)
Ballee Primary School, Ballymena

Anger

Anger is red like Wayne Rooney throwing his boots down
When he got substituted
Anger sounds like a roaring wind blowing away the summer leaves
On the big, tall trees
Anger tastes like spicy curry chicken running down my throat
Anger smells like chilli peppers cooking in the saucepan
Anger feels like teachers nagging on and on
Anger reminds me of lava erupting from a volcano.

Geoffrey Dunlop (10)
Ballee Primary School, Ballymena

Fear

Fear is black like getting trapped in a deep hole
Fear sounds like growling thunder on a stormy day
Fear smells like stuffing on a Sunday dinner
Fear tastes like crispy lettuce, yum-yum
Fear looks like crackling lightning, *bang!* as it hits the ground
Fear feels like my heart pumping with horror
Fear reminds me of how I feel when my dog tries to bite me.

James Douglas (10)
Ballee Primary School, Ballymena

Happiness

Happiness is yellow shining in the sun
Happiness sounds like runny egg sizzling in the pan
Happiness tastes like vanilla ice cream melting in my mouth
Happiness looks like a big sandy beach
Happiness smells like a sunflower growing in the sun
Happiness feels like a big yellow teddy bear sitting on my bed.

Rebecca Hempsey (10)
Ballee Primary School, Ballymena

Hate

Hate feels like raspberry juice flowing through your hands
Hate tastes like a hot kettle in your mouth
Hate smells like a rotten egg
Hate looks like a stream of lava flowing out of the volcano
It reminds me of the Liverpool home kit.

Paul Bell (10)
Ballee Primary School, Ballymena

Happiness

Happiness is yellow like the sun in the clear blue sky
It sounds like smoked bacon sizzling in the pan
It smells like sweet summer air
It looks like the coloured leaves dangling off the tree
It feels like the big yellow sun touching the back of my legs
It tastes like buns just out of the oven
It reminds me of ripe bananas in Australia.

Daniel Bainbridge (10)
Ballee Primary School, Ballymena

Fear

Red is my colour
It sounds like your heart beating louder and louder
It tastes like hot, strong curry
It smells like rotting animal flesh
It looks like a hairy-scary Hallowe'en mask
It feels like spikes on a hedgehog's back
It reminds me of people stealing my phone.

Joseph Nixon (10)
Ballee Primary School, Ballymena

Anger

Anger sounds like bacon sizzling in the pan
Anger tastes like burning burgers on the barbeque
Anger smells like red-hot chilli peppers
Anger looks like an exploding volcano
It reminds me of the bonfire.

Carson Boyd (10)
Ballee Primary School, Ballymena

Happiness

Happiness is like grapes growing on the vine
It sounds like horses playing in the field
It tastes like watermelon dripping in my mouth
It smells like lavender drooping from a bush
It looks like playful kittens playing with balls of yarn
It feels like feathers running down my cheek
It reminds me of bowls of fruit.

Naomi Doherty (10)
Ballee Primary School, Ballymena

The Vikings Are Coming!

The Vikings are coming!
Hear their slashing swords!
Swinging the wind our way!
Run, run, run!

The Vikings are coming!
Hear them bellow!
Shouting at us!
Get away, get away!

The Vikings are coming!
See the ship's prow!
Closer and closer they come!
The Vikings are coming!

Jack Thompson (9)
Enniskillen Model Primary School, Enniskillen

Autumn

Autumn is coming
Leaves are blowing and swirling
Chestnuts and conkers are falling
The wind is blowing
And the blackberries are out.

Bright red juicy apples are out
And lots of colourful leaves
The birds are migrating
And the animals are hibernating.

Autumn is coming
The mist is out
The leaves are falling from the trees
The leaves are swirling and twirling
And the farmers are harvesting their crops.

Emma Nixon (9)
Enniskillen Model Primary School, Enniskillen

The Vikings Are Coming!

The Vikings are coming
To fight with us.
They are coming by a big, scary ship
Not by an old, smelly bus.

The Vikings are coming
I wish they would go away.
But I know that they're
Not here to go
And they are not here to play.

I know that the Vikings are at my front door
But I'd just like to say.
The Vikings are coming
This very day.

Luke Todd (9)
Enniskillen Model Primary School, Enniskillen

Autumn

A is for nice, juicy apples hanging on the trees
U is for umbrellas when the days are wet
T is for tortoises getting ready to hibernate
U is for underground moles sleeping
M is for mist that comes when it's dark
N is for nature around you and me.

Mark Haskins (10)
Enniskillen Model Primary School, Enniskillen

My Identity

My name is Harry McCurry
I'm very tall and slim, aged nine
My mum says I'm always in a hurry
To play football so I can get on that goal line

My favourite team is Man U
My brother Alexander's Liverpool
As for my sister, Annie-Lou
She doesn't care at all, but that's cool

I live near the aerodrome
And when I'm not in drum school
It's up and down Devenish Lane I roam
Or else I'm having fun and acting the fool

I'm a P6 pupil at the Model
My teacher's Mrs Logan
The work is sure no doddle
But if I work hard, I'll get a token.

Harry McCurry (9)
Enniskillen Model Primary School, Enniskillen

Autumn

A is for juicy apples hanging in the apple trees
U is for umbrellas that keep us dry in the autumn rain
T is for trees which lose their leaves in the autumn
U is for underground where the hedgehogs sleep
M is for mist which covers the morning sky
N is for nature which we see every day.

James Abraham (9)
Enniskillen Model Primary School, Enniskillen

Autumn

Leaves, leaves, leaves
Falling off the trees
Twirling round and round
Swirling round and round

Leaves, leaves, leaves
Changing different colours
Red, yellow, brown
What colour will be next?

Leaves, leaves, leaves
Please tell me, please
Which leaf will fall next?
One, two or three?

Caroline Murphy (9)
Enniskillen Model Primary School, Enniskillen

Me

Me oh my
I have some friends
Who are really wild!
Me oh my

Me oh my
I'm almost ten
30th of October
I'm hanging with my friends

Me oh my
Football's on!
Come on and play!
For it's our team today!

Me oh my
Music I prefer
Than sitting on a chair!

Me oh my
It's the end of the day
Better rush
Or I'll be late today!

Emma Shaw (9)
Enniskillen Model Primary School, Enniskillen

My Identity

My name is Adam
I am no madam

I love football
But always fall

I'm only nine
But I drink wine

My friend Lee
Is smaller than me

My brothers
Will never have
Different mothers

I like blues
Of all different hues

I love the wrestler Sting
But hate really stupid things

I love 'Fifa Street'
But hate eating meat

I love eating crackers
But hate seeing smackers

I love 'South Park'
But hate hearing dogs bark.

Adam Carson (9)
Enniskillen Model Primary School, Enniskillen

Me

Here I am!
There's just one of me,
All of my friends are different from me,
I have green eyes and a button nose,
That's me!

Here I am!
Yes, I go to school,
My favourite subject is English,
I have a fab teacher, who is wonderful,
I have some great friends, who are so cool.

Here I am!
And my favourite food,
Is pizza, garlic bread with Coke,
With ice cream for afters,
On a Friday night,
It's really hard to beat!

Here I am!
My favourite pop band is McFly!
Their music is just great,
My hobbies are reading, knitting and drawing
And my life is full and I feel great,
That's me!

Courteney Moore (9)
Enniskillen Model Primary School, Enniskillen

Me

Me, oh my, what can I see?
Tall, not small
Wise like an owl
Fast like a hare
Or maybe swimming like a frog
Or at home playing with my dog
Being silly like a monkey.
My favourite hobbies are football and riding my bike
My favourite subject is maths
I am magnificent at that.
My birthday's the 9th of June
My favourite sports are football and the Olympics
My favourite music is rock music
My favourite food is pizza.

Aaron Coalter (9)
Enniskillen Model Primary School, Enniskillen

My Identity

My name is Sophie
And I live in a sock
It is so spotty
I love it so much

My name is Sophie
And no one's like me
I play with my friends
And no one else

My name is Sophie
And I am nine
I am tall
And I play football

My name is Sophie
I have no pets
I would like one
But not just yet.

Sophie Jordan (9)
Enniskillen Model Primary School, Enniskillen

My Identity

J umping all the time
U seful
D igging all the time
I ntelligent
T alkative
H appy

C aring for people
A nimal crazy
T umbling around
H appy
C haritable
A good listener
R espectful
T errific.

Judith Cathcart (9)
Enniskillen Model Primary School, Enniskillen

Habitats

Lions roar and growl
Somewhere in the savannah
Gazelles skip and jump
Somewhere in the savannah.

Jaguars leap from trees above
Somewhere in the jungle
Macaws squawk and flap through the trees
Somewhere in the jungle.

Dolphins chatter and click
Somewhere in the sea
Fish swim and splash
Somewhere in the sea.

Penguins slide on their tums
Somewhere on an icy land
Artic foxes so white you cannot see
Somewhere on an icy land.

Rabbits hop
Somewhere on Fair Isle
Sheep baa
Somewhere on Fair Isle.

Erin Welch (11)
Fair Isle Primary School, Shetland

Flowers

Flowers grow,
Flowers grow everywhere,
Hey! There's one over there!
You grow them in your garden,
You see them everywhere,
You grow them in pots,
You see them in the forest.

Melissa Welch (7)
Fair Isle Primary School, Shetland

The Animals In My Hall

Horses honking,
Cows clonking,
Owls swooping,
Dogs snooping,
Cats jumping in the air,
Don't go in there, there's a bear!

Lions roaring,
Eagles soaring,
Porcupine pricking,
Frogs sticking,
But the weirdest thing of all
Are the animals in my hall!

Amy Stout (11)
Fair Isle Primary School, Shetland

Did You See The Puffin?

Did you see the puffin?
Did you see the muffin?
Did you see the disappearing muffin?
If you didn't see the disappearing muffin,
It was eaten by the puffin!

Oliver Harrison (9)
Fair Isle Primary School, Shetland

An Ode To Steve Irwin

There was a croc hunter called Steve
He did things you wouldn't believe
He fought spiders and snakes
And piranhas in lakes
He had lots of tricks up his sleeve.

Steve, he built a big zoo
He may have even built two
But one day in the ocean
A stingray caused a commotion
And now Steve is gone - sad, but true.

Sean Austin (8)
Lourdes Primary School, Carrickfergus

Harvey

I have a dog called Harvey
His colour's white and brown
He loves to chase his ball
Running all around

I have a dog called Harvey
He loves it by the sea
He jumps into the water
Splashing over me

I have a dog called Harvey
I love him, oh so dear
He always wags his tail at me
Whenever I go near

Each time I throw his ball for him
He brings it back to me
And when it's time to have his tea
I'm sure I see him smile

I have a dog called Harvey
My friend, my chum, my pal.

Victoria McKendrick (8)
Lourdes Primary School, Carrickfergus

Wintertime

Wintertime, wintertime,
Storms and rain,
It's just the opposite
Of sunny Spain.

I lie in my bed,
All shivering and blue,
If I don't wear my jammies,
I might catch the flu.

It's fun to make snowmen
And play in the snow,
All wrapped up cosily,
While the north wind does blow.

Oh, how I like winter
'Cause Santa Claus comes
And we leave him out
Some hot cross buns.

I wake up in the morning,
All happy to see,
My presents before me,
Wrapped under the tree!

Luke Herdman (9)
Lourdes Primary School, Carrickfergus

My Garden

Just last week we moved to a new home
The garden is very big, with lots of room to roam
My sister, Kate and me are as happy as can be
We love it when Granny and Granda stay with us for tea
My friend came to visit me and we went to explore
When a big, brown bull saw us and it began to roar
We ran home very, very fast
And hid behind the kitchen door until the bull had passed.

Peter Shannon (8)
Lourdes Primary School, Carrickfergus

My Dad's Paintbox

One day my dad said,
'Would you like to see my paintbox?'

Yellow is the bright sun
Blue is the cold, icy sea
Purple is a big, juicy plum
Red is a warm, blazing fire
Pink is a little girl's frilly dress
Green is the tall trees blowing in the wind
Orange is the peaceful sunset
Brown is tasty chocolate in my mouth
Black is the sleek cat at night.

Olivia Lennox (9)
Lourdes Primary School, Carrickfergus

Spider-Man

S uper human, saving people
P aranormal man, jumping from steeples
I ndestructable, can't be crushed
D eath-defying stuntman, won't fall in the dust
E nergetic super-spider, eternal combat man
R ed daredevil, better than Batman

M issionary fighting to overcome crime
A mazing arachnid, clearing up slime
N o wonder he's the best!

Matthew Murray (11)
Lourdes Primary School, Carrickfergus

In The Kitchen!

In the kitchen I can hear the phone ringing,
I can also hear my sister singing,
I can smell the lovely food,
It really does smell so good.

I talk about my day at school
And going to the swimming pool,
I can see the plates and dishes,
Piled high with chips and fishes.

My mum gives off for using my hands,
The bangs and crashes of pots and pans,
My dad cracks terrible jokes,
Starts to laugh and then he chokes.

My brother plonks down on his seat,
He really loves to eat and eat,
Cutlery clatters to the floor,
This place is mad, I'm out the door!

Bronagh Stewart (11)
Lourdes Primary School, Carrickfergus

Winter

Winter is my favourite season
Here are my many reasons
The colours looks so crisp and sharp
I love it when it's cold and dark
The snow falls like little stars
It covers all the motor cars

Santa comes on Christmas Day
He leaves our presents and goes away
I get up to see what he has left
Going quietly, holding my breath
I love the winter, snow and ice
A time so cold, a time so nice.

Katie McKendrick (10)
Lourdes Primary School, Carrickfergus

Football Crazy

F is for footie, the fun game
O is for our opponents
O is for those who are sent off
T is for my team
B is the best
A is for athletes
L is for league
L is for lobbing the keeper

Football is my dream!

Matthew Maguire (10)
Lourdes Primary School, Carrickfergus

Summer Sailing

In summertime I like to sail
With my good friend, Jack.
We race each other in our boats
Around the course and back.

I love to sail out on the sea
And sometimes go quite fast.
It's fun to race with other boats
And I'm glad I don't come last!

But summertime is over now
No more sailing for me.
Until next year when once again
I can sail out on the sea.

Pierce Woods (9)
Lourdes Primary School, Carrickfergus

Happiness

Happiness to me is multicoloured
It sounds like my favourite popstar playing on the radio
It tastes like freshly baked buns
It looks like a colourful explosion of fireworks
It feels like a silk sheet covering me
It feels like I am dancing forever
It smells like the fresh spring air
I feel so happy!

Ciara McCabe (10)
Lourdes Primary School, Carrickfergus

Rathlin Island

Rathlin is an island
In the middle of the sea.

Most of the people who live there
Are related to me.

I love to run around the fields
And chase the rabbits and sheep,
To fish in the ports
And swim in the strand.

Then head up to the caravan
For a nice, cosy sleep.

David Glanville Reid (10)
Lourdes Primary School, Carrickfergus

Poetry Happiness

Fear's colour is red
Fear tastes like black mud
Fear smells like rotten dead people
Fear looks like something dying
Fear sounds like a woman screeching
Fear feels like a spike up your back
Fear hurts me

Happiness' colour is orange
Happiness tastes like light strawberry cakes
Happiness smells like the perfume Dior
Happiness looks like pink tulips
Happiness sounds like a party going on
Happiness feels like a great big fiesta

Love's colour is light purple
Loves tastes like the kind of chocolates your boyfriend gives you
Love smells like an orchid
Love looks like a love that cannot be broken
Love sounds like a bird chirping
Love feels like you don't want to let go.

Katie Gordon (11)
Mill O' Forest Primary School, Stonehaven

Emotions

Fear is the darkest black
Fear tastes like a bitter sweet covered in slime
And smells like rotting bodies
Fear looks like a black oblivion waiting to consume you
Fear makes me nervous

Love is the brightest blue
It tastes like chocolate ice cream
And smells like the tallest daffodil
Love is like the sun waiting to warm you
And sounds like a laughing child
Love makes me feel happy

Depression is the saddest red
It tastes like cold stones in your mouth
And smells like rotting broccoli in a pan of grease
Depression is like a pair of cold, bony hands reaching for you
It feels like fear.

Angus Matheson (11)
Mill O' Forest Primary School, Stonehaven

Emotions

Frustration is dark red
It tastes like trying to eat lemons
And smells like sweat
Frustration looks like pushing a 10,000kg weight
Worst of all, it feels like a huge wave crashing down on me
Frustration makes me shiver

Jealousy is minty-green
It tastes like sour milk
And smells like rotten fruit
Jealousy looks like fire
Worst of all, it feels like someone is always bullying you
Jealousy makes me fight

Loneliness is black
It tastes like bitter fruit juice
And smells like a cold, damp room
Loneliness looks like nothing
Worst of all, it feels like nobody cares about you
Loneliness makes me sad.

Kieran Johnson (11)
Mill O' Forest Primary School, Stonehaven

Mixed Emotions

Depression is a deep black colour
It tastes like dirt
It smells like a fire
Depression looks like a black, cold heart
It sounds like thumping music
And it makes me feel mentally ill

Love is a golden pink colour
It tastes like chocolate doughnuts
Love smells of roses
It feels like the hands of a newborn baby
It sounds of soft music
Love looks like a bed of roses

Happiness is a blue colour
It tastes like cookies
And smells of wine
It looks like newborn lion cubs
It sounds like laughter
My most happiest time is with my friend on my trampoline.

Rachael Craig (11)
Mill O' Forest Primary School, Stonehaven

My Personal Feelings

Sadness
Sadness is blue like a river
It tastes like a tear from my eye
Sadness sounds like a drip from a tap
And looks like an overflowing bath
When I think of sadness, it makes me feel upset

Happiness
Happiness is the colour of a rainbow
And it tastes like a sweet lollipop
Happiness sounds like a joyful laugh
It looks like a smile on your face
When I think of happiness, it puts a smile on my face

Fear
Fear is the colour of a silver padlock
It tastes like a bitter lemon
Fear sounds like ice cracking
And it looks like a glittering ice cube
When I think of fear, it reminds me of spiders.

Victoria Paisley (11)
Mill O' Forest Primary School, Stonehaven

Emotions

Fear, love and hate

Fear is white
And tastes like a bitter lemon
It smells like sweat running off your forehead
Fear looks like a ghost jumping in front of you
Fear sounds like a train going past you at full speed
It feels like somebody scaring you 24/7

Love is red
Loves tastes like the finest food
It tastes like a red rose
And looks like two people on a park bench
Love sounds like a love song on the radio
It feels like you forget things

Hate is black
Hate tastes like dirty food
It smells like a dead body
And looks like a face, steam coming out of its ears
Hate sounds like rubbish music
Hate feels like somebody kicking you.

Lee Ramage (11)
Mill O' Forest Primary School, Stonehaven

Emotions

Stress is the colour grey
It tastes of bitter lime
The smell is of mouldy rats
It looks like someone pulling out their hair
It sounds like a scream
It feels like the top of a glue stick
Stress makes me feel weird

Yellow is the colour of happiness
Happiness tastes like chocolate
Happiness smells like lavender
Happiness looks like people playing
Happiness sounds like everyone talking nicely
Happiness feels like flowers
Happiness makes me feel glad

Love is the colour rosy red
Love tastes like fresh grapes
Love smells like pine
Love looks like a rose
Love sounds like a love song
Love feels like a petal
Love makes me feel good.

Michael Blacklaw (11)
Mill O' Forest Primary School, Stonehaven

Emotional Thoughts

Anger
Anger is as black as night
It tastes like mouldy meat
And smells of cheese gone bad
It looks like muddy feet
Anger sounds like thundering lightning
And feels like a ruined day
Anger makes me feel sad

Happiness
Happiness is a light, bright blue
It tastes like chocolate cake
And smells like washing powder
It looks like a trip to the moon
Happiness sounds like a birthday song
It feels like a splendid achievement
Happiness makes me laugh

Fear
Fear is a dark purple
And it tastes like salt
It smells of wild rats
And looks like grey clouds
Fear sounds like screaming
Fear makes me scared.

Caitlin Milne (11)
Mill O' Forest Primary School, Stonehaven

Emotions

Joy is green
It tastes like hot fudge pudding
And smells like a rose on a summer's day
Joy looks like a freshly cut meadow
It sounds like a bird singing in the morning
Joy is pleasure

Depression is blue
It tastes like raw meat
The smell is like burnt cabbage
Depression looks like a sad child in his room
It sounds like moaning and screaming
Depression is boring

Anger is black
And tastes like metal fresh from a fire
It smells like dirt from a graveyard
Anger looks like coal on a fire
The sound is like a beanbag dummy ripping
Anger is not my favourite.

Sam Jones-Lawman (11)
Mill O' Forest Primary School, Stonehaven

Mixed Emotions

Love is red
It tastes like strawberry chocolates
And smells like red roses
Love looks like two people cuddling
It sounds like wonderful love music
Love makes me feel like forgetting things

Hate is jet-black
It tastes like bitter lemon
And smells like rotten eggs
Hate looks like a dark stormy night
It sounds like thunder and lightning
Hate feels like trickling blood

Happiness is bright orange
It tastes like sweet strawberries
And smells like yellow flowers
Happiness looks like friends playing together
It sounds like laughter and giggles
Happiness feels outstanding.

Stuart Moir (10)
Mill O' Forest Primary School, Stonehaven

My Personal Thoughts

Anger
Anger is as black as night
And tastes like a mouldy chocolate bar
It smells of blown-up lights
And looks like a damaged car
It sounds like thunder in the night
And feels like melted tar
Anger leaves me with no light

Sadness
Sadness is as blue as a stream
It tastes of bitter lemons
And smells of steam
It looks like cannons
And sounds like boring old teens
It feels like a burning tan
Sadness makes me mean

Fear
Fear is as white as snow
And tastes of mould
It smells of cows
And looks like men really old
It sounds like ploughs
And feels like slimy toads
Fear is like thunderclouds.

Rebecca Yvonne Watt (11)
Mill O' Forest Primary School, Stonehaven

Emotions - Love, Happiness And Fear

Love is a baby pink colour
Tasting of chocolate cake
Smelling like roses, red, pink and white
Looking like a yellow cottage with a garden of flowers
Sounding like laughter and not a care in the world
It feels like the time I went with my family to fly a new kite

Happiness is blue in colour
Tasting of muffins
Smelling of cakes baking
Looking like a newly finished biscuit I'd been making
Sounding like a baby chick chirping
Feeling like the time my kitten came home

Fear is as black as night
Tasting of saltwater
Smelling of fire, getting closer and closer
Looking like a very fierce fight
Sounding like a leopard, as he is killed by a lion
Feeling like you are alone in a dark room.

Shannon Smith (11)
Mill O' Forest Primary School, Stonehaven

Love, Hate And Sadness

Love is a sweet candy pink
It tastes like bubblegum flavoured lipgloss
It smells like freshly washed pillows
And looks like a newly wed couple
It sounds like bluebirds singing in the trees
Love makes me feel heavenly

Hate is fire engine red
The flavour of hate is the metallic blood dribbling down my chin
It smells like spicy chicken tikka
Hate looks like my sister using up my new nail varnish
And hates makes me stomp up the stairs and grit my teeth

Sadness is a pale, baby blue
And tastes like the mascara that's dribbled off my eyes
and down my cheek
It smells like my dad's aftershave after hugging him
And looks like all my friends breaking up
Sadness sounds like a weeping dog
And it feels like guilt rushing through the cold blood in my body.

Kimberly Dickie (11)
Mill O' Forest Primary School, Stonehaven

Touching Emotions

Anger
Anger is fiery red
It tastes like sour milk
And smells of old socks and depression
Anger looks like an unwanted child
The sound of ghostly ghosts giggling
Anger frightens me

Love
Love is shimmering pink
It tastes of strawberries and cream
Love smells of expensive perfumes
It looks like a mushy couple in the park
Love sounds like animals waking up in the morning
Love makes me laugh

Sadness
Sadness is glittering blue
It tastes of salty tears
And smells of a dinner left for two
Sadness looks like the grave of a close relative
The sound of crying animals
Sadness makes me weep!

Kirsty Thomson (11)
Mill O' Forest Primary School, Stonehaven

Emotions!

Fear is red
It tastes like Brussels sprouts
And smells like rotten fruit
It looks like something old and disgusting
And sounds like doors creaking
It feels like cold snow
Fear makes me nervous

Anger is orange
It tastes like broccoli
And smells like garbage left for ages
It looks like dead fish
And sounds like yourself shouting
It feels like a hot iron
Anger makes me want to be alone

Hate is yellow
It tastes like sweetcorn
And smells like manure
It looks like an overflowing dustbin
And sounds like someone talking under their breath
It feels like the temperature has gone up
Hate makes me want to eat junk food!

Ryan Campbell (11)
Mill O' Forest Primary School, Stonehaven

Emotions

Fear is white
It tastes like a very bitter lemon
And smells like a piece of rotten meat
Fear looks like someone falling from a great height
And sounds like a very high-pitched scream
Fear makes me scared

Happiness is bright yellow
And tastes like red apples
It smells like bright flowers and a red rose
Happiness looks like lots of people playing together
And it sounds like children talking happily
Happiness feels great

Hate is dark black
It tastes like dead rats
And smells like mouldy cheese
Hate looks like someone murdering an innocent person
And it sounds like people shouting at everyone
Hate is horrible.

Jason Kelly (10)
Mill O' Forest Primary School, Stonehaven

Emotions

Happiness
Happiness is bright yellow
And tastes like a ripe red apple
Happiness smells like a rosy red rose
And looks like a yellow star in the night sky
Happiness sounds like a little sheep baaing
Happiness feels like a big lump of toffee in your mouth

Love
Love is rosy red
Love tastes like a small, plump peach
Love smells like a sniff of perfume
Love looks like melted chocolate
Love sounds like a hummingbird
Love feels like a Malteser melting in your mouth

Joy
Joy is light blue
And tastes like a nice yellow banana
Joy smells like a field of poppies
And looks like a nice, small calf
Joy sounds like the church bells ringing
And feels like a back massage.

Jonathan Penman (11)
Mill O' Forest Primary School, Stonehaven

My Weird Family

My mum is insane
My dad's even worse
He goes around town, wearing Donald Duck T-shirts!
My sister is crazy
She sleeps in parks!
I don't want to talk about my brother, he's even worse
He will only go to school in pants!
My baby brother is not so bad
But I wish he wasn't born in hay
I wish he would go away
He burps in the night, leaving a little curse
But my dad is still the worst!

Rebecca Turner (8)
Mill O' Forest Primary School, Stonehaven

All About Me

My name is Bethany Nicol
I am a little girl
My hair is fair and straight
It doesn't have a curl

My favourite hobby's dancing
I play piano too
I'm also good at swimming
I have so much to do

Then there's all my homework
To be handed in on Thursday
When it gets to Friday
I shout, hip hip hooray!

I've got three older brothers
Then there's Mum and Dad
I haven't got a sister
For that, I'm really glad!

I love all my friends and family
My life is very good
I wouldn't change a single thing
Even if I could!

Bethany Nicol (9)
Mill O' Forest Primary School, Stonehaven

Billy

There once was a boy called Billy,
Who had a sister called Milly,
They played with Bart
And ate strawberry tart,
But then the weather turned chilly.

Amy Robertson (9)
Mill O' Forest Primary School, Stonehaven

My Dog

My name is Chelsea
And I have a dog called Spike
He is not very fate
And he likes to flap
And wrap himself in a map
He likes his food, because it's good
He likes to go mad in the garden

He is very small, with a little call
He likes to lay in the sun, with a bun
He likes to go for a walk
And wears a sock
He's scared of cats, because they scratch
And I love him loads!

Chelsea Lobban (9)
Mill O' Forest Primary School, Stonehaven

About Pets

I have a cat called Fudge
Who has a sister called Smudge
Fudge sleeps all day
While Smudge goes out to play.

I have a dog called Seth
Who has a sister called Beth
Seth goes to the park
And Beth likes to bark.

I have a parrot called Polly
Who has a sister called Molly
Polly likes to speak
And Molly plays hide-and-seek.

I have a pony called Billy
Who has a sister called Milly
Billy is silly
And so is Milly.

I have a fish called Ted
Who has a sister called Red
Ted likes to go fast
And Red is always last.

Beth Johnson (9)
Mill O' Forest Primary School, Stonehaven

My Cat

My name is Anna
And I have a cat
His name is Rolo
And he's not very fat
He likes to go outside
And play in the trees
But a very strange thing is
He likes to eat cheese!

He's stripy and fluffy
With a very long tail
He won't go outside
When there's a gale
He lies in the sun
When it is hot
He is my cat
And I love him a lot!

Anna Jenneson (9)
Mill O' Forest Primary School, Stonehaven

Hallowe'en

One day on Hallowe'en,
It was very scary,
I saw a werewolf,
Who was very hairy!

I went to Hogwarts
And saw a key with a wing,
Then all of the students,
Began to sing, sing, sing!

Then I went
To trick or treat,
Where I saw a zombie,
Eating fresh pig meat.

And then I went home,
To see my mum,
Who was busy drinking,
Lots of rum!

Jack Neill (8)
Mill O' Forest Primary School, Stonehaven

Oscar The Ogre

Oscar the ogre, what a happy soul!
Unlike his brother who's very sad and old.
One day Oscar went to see his brother,
So he went to his house but he met his mother.
She told Oscar his brother had gone out,
But then she had a heart attack and even passed out.
They rushed to the hospital and she had her heart checked,
Then they rushed back home again, but the house was wrecked.
Mr Muffin saw nothing, Mrs Glenathin didn't see anything,
So no one knows what happened.

Mark Leith (9)
Mill O' Forest Primary School, Stonehaven

Freddy

There once was a cat called Freddy
He liked to sleep on my beddy
He was no use at rat catching
But great at bat hatching
And was a cry kitty if he hadn't got my teddy.

He came for his food at bedtime
Then got a pat in the morning
And went back to sleep at lunchtime
He never got to play
Just slept inside all day.

Lauren Smith (9)
Mill O' Forest Primary School, Stonehaven

A Ghost

A ghost is scary, spooky and sly
Sleeps under your bed and spooks you at night
He freaks you as well when he calls your name
His real home is a graveyard - black and plain
He hides in it sometimes
But not all day
But he thinks he's so funny
But really he's not
And that's why I hate him a lot!

Tegan Wilson (9)
Mill O' Forest Primary School, Stonehaven

The Man In The Navy

There once was a man from the navy
Who love to eat chicken and gravy
His pet chicken he ate
He said it was great
And now he keeps a cow called Davy.

Cameron Pyper (9)
Mill O' Forest Primary School, Stonehaven

A Tin

There once was a girl called A Tin
Who had just one very long fin
She swam underwater
With her very fat daughter
And then she swan into the bin!

Lyndsay Clark (10)
Mill O' Forest Primary School, Stonehaven

Dex And His Specs

There once was a man called Dex
He had some very large specs
They were the size of a dog
And they glowed in the fog
And now they have shrunk his neck!

Jemma Campbell (9)
Mill O' Forest Primary School, Stonehaven

Big Fish

There once was a very big fish
I used to keep it in a dish
One day he got bitten
By a big fluffy kitten
So he disappeared with a swish!

Ashleigh Mackay (9)
Mill O' Forest Primary School, Stonehaven

The Girl Who Fell In A Stream

There once was a girl from Aberdeen
Who was always living in a dream
She daydreamed all day
Had no time to play
And one day she fell in a stream!

Jodie Kirk (9)
Mill O' Forest Primary School, Stonehaven

Green As Can Be

There once was a girl from Dundee
Who hit her head on a tree
To hospital she went
Her bone was bent
And now she is as green as can be!

Paige Howey (8)
Mill O' Forest Primary School, Stonehaven

War

War is horrible
Makes me think of fear
Death, tears and injuries
And bombs destroying things
Just imagine an air raid in the middle of the night
Everybody rushing for shelter in terror and fright.

Nicole Johnston (11)
Mill O' Forest Primary School, Stonehaven

War

War is a disaster
Please, no more wars.

People die
But survivors cry.

Please be friends
And that's how this poem ends!

Michael Dunlop (11)
Mill O' Forest Primary School, Stonehaven

Clever Seal

When I went to the Falkirk Wheel,
I really think I saw a seal,
He looked so very grey and old,
When I looked at him, my blood ran cold.

He looked at me with his big, grey eyes,
Then I threw him a bucket of pies,
He ate them all as fast as ever
And I thought he was very clever!

Kelsey Stewart (9)
Mill O' Forest Primary School, Stonehaven

The Man From Kent

There once was a man from Kent
Who always lived in a tent
A lion came one day
A sunny day in May
And ate up the man as he went!

Amy Gillies (9)
Mill O' Forest Primary School, Stonehaven

Spotty Man

There was a young man from France
Who collected old, spotty pants
He washed them and dyed them
And then he dried them
For the big foxtrot dance!

Alana Nicol (10)
Mill O' Forest Primary School, Stonehaven

The Daydreaming Girl

There once was a girl who always dreamed,
Of horses and ponies and bumblebees,
She never, ever finished her work,
She always was a one to lurk,
At home she wasn't that much better,
She couldn't even post a letter,
Without dreaming and falling over,
She really needs a four-leaf clover.

Emma Hunter (9)
Mill O' Forest Primary School, Stonehaven

The Baby And The Cow

Once there was a lightning storm,
Just before a baby was born,
Then he started screaming so,
Now he listens to the radio.

He is a lot older now
And he looks after a cow,
Then the cow said a little word
And he accidentally overheard.

Robert Barry Cruickshank (9)
Mill O' Forest Primary School, Stonehaven

The Man And The Rat

There once was a man that was fat
And wanted an old, big rat
He got one, you see
But it bit him on the knee
And they both fell onto a mat.

Liam Ferries (10)
Mill O' Forest Primary School, Stonehaven

Star, My Dog

Please don't start to bawl and shout,
Just read my letter and hear me out.
I come from a farm at the end of a track,
Please look after me, don't send me back.
Four brothers and three sisters, I'm the last of the litter
People say I'm the runt, but I'm not bitter.
Mum and Dad at work all day,
Seven of us were left to run and play.
My brothers and sister left, one by one,
I'm all alone now, not much fun.
Five, ten, fifteen years in a loving home,
Don't put me out on the streets to roam.
I would like to be in a house of fun,
Not on a farm in an old dog run.
I won't take much looking after
And can bring you joy and laughter.
I will try not to be wild and bad,
Cos I'm only looking for a mum and dad.
They say I can't be with working dogs
And call me just plain Joe Bloggs.
If I could go with you in the car,
I'd wag my tail and be a star.
I've pled my case and done my best,
It's up to you to decide the rest.
If you decide to care for me,
Hip hip hooray, I'll see my first Christmas tree.

Rebekah Laing (9)
Mill O' Forest Primary School, Stonehaven

Come On And Celebrate

Acting is fun, acting is great
Let's go to acting to celebrate
I really enjoy it, yes I do,
I just love acting, what about you?
Come along and you'll meet a mate or two!

Cara Findlay (10)
Mill O' Forest Primary School, Stonehaven

My Perfect Light

My candle burns at both ends,
It will not last the night.
Ah, but to all my friends and all my foes,
It gives a lovely light.
The night is weak,
But my story is not complete.
My candle is out now,
But I am glad I know not to be sad.

Roddyne Mentiplay (9)
Mill O' Forest Primary School, Stonehaven

The Girl From Dundee

There once was a girl from Dundee
Who fell on top of a bee,
She fell over a chair
And pulled out her hair
Then went home and had some tea.

Stephanie Mair (10)
Mill O' Forest Primary School, Stonehaven

The Baby And The Gravy

My auntie and uncle had a cute baby
By accident, it fell in the gravy
They squished it and squashed it
And mashed it and mushed it
When she found it, my auntie went crazy.

Brodie Cummins (9)
Mill O' Forest Primary School, Stonehaven

Princesses

P erfect people dressed up in robes
R iding in carriages, waving about their hands
I n the palace they dress in fine clothes
N ow look out of your window, your prince awaits
C limb out of your window and down the vine
E verybody wonders what's for tea, why, it's bread and wine
S inging in the highest pitch
S inging in the lowest pitch
E verybody enjoying themselves
S weet and wonderful princesses, dancing in the wind.

Catherine Ritchie (9)
Mill O' Forest Primary School, Stonehaven

War In World War II

Worried, worried,
Bombs exploding,
Worried people,
Tanks and Germans,
Guns, sirens and evacuation too.
Children laughing,
Running, crying,
Wailing for survival,
Winning, winning!

Tonicha Masson (10)
Mill O' Forest Primary School, Stonehaven

War

During World War II there were a lot of explosions
Children evacuated from cities to the countryside
The air raid sirens terrified children
And the sound of bombs as they hit their targets
Everywhere rubble, death and destruction
What is the purpose of war?

Connor Douglas (10)
Mill O' Forest Primary School, Stonehaven

Tragic War

World War II was so devastating
Bombs were dropping
    Planes were crashing
Explosions were happening
    And blackouts were blackening
Gas masks were worn
    And children were
  Gone!

Kim Mellis (11)
Mill O' Forest Primary School, Stonehaven

War

Old Mrs Myren
Set off the siren
Me and Mr Belter
Run for the shelter

But wait!
We've forgotten our little mate
He's sitting at home, playing in a crate
We run along, shouting, 'Tom!'
We hope he hasn't been hit by a bomb

We've found him now
He's safe, we're glad
This war has made us very sad.

Sean Leith (10)
Mill O' Forest Primary School, Stonehaven

Night War

I'm sleeping in bed, safe and sound,
The sirens go off,
They are loud,
The Germans are coming,
Get to the shelter,
Outside is freezing,
The blackout has started,
We cannot see a thing,
They are dropping more and more bombs,
I hear one big bomb,
I hear tanks, planes, guns and bombs overhead,
The worst bit of all
Is when we hear death,
I call this night -
War!

Jack Spence (11)
Mill O' Forest Primary School, Stonehaven

What Boys And Girls Are Made Of

Boys are made of dumb stuff
And dull colours and all boring stuff
Girls are made of exciting stuff, gossip, girly talk
And everything you think girls are made of
Mums are made of love and joy
And sometimes are full of frightening poison
Last of all, what are dads made of?
Fun and energy and sometimes as scary as a ghost.

Heather Gerrard (9)
Mill O' Forest Primary School, Stonehaven

A Spooky Owl!

In the middle of the night,
I heard a creak,
It was wild! It was crazy!
But what could it be?
I turned around and there sat an owl, sitting on a branch,
'Boo! I have got you now,' the owl said, hanging onto me,
I got frightened!
It was really spooky,
I ran into the house, it was red, blue and haunted
And I thought the owl might hurt me badly,
But it didn't, it just wanted to be my friend,
The owl could talk,
So we both played a board game,
It was called, 'A Class Person',
The colour of the owl was black, brown and white.

Serena Masson (9)
Mill O' Forest Primary School, Stonehaven

The Bat

One night,
I had a fright,
A big, hairy bat,
It turned into a cat
And then it stared at me,
I didn't know what it could be,
But then I thought, a bat of course,
But not a horse,
Definitely not,
It jumped an awful lot,
You will find it where people never go,
Yes of course, in the snow!

Katie Cruickshank (8)
Mill O' Forest Primary School, Stonehaven

My Granny's Scarf

My granny's scarf was fluffy
And also very stuffy,
She told me it was old,
I was sad to know,
The colour of it was white,
It was very bright,
It looked like a kite,
In the sunlight.

When the scarf is round my belly,
I watch the telly,
My granny's scarf was as light as a kite,
So that's my granny's scarf alright,
As bright as a kite in the sunlight,
Alright!

Megan Robertson (9)
Mill O' Forest Primary School, Stonehaven

Watch Out!

Watch out, he bites,
He will catch you in the night,
Now watch out, you will get a fright,
Watch out, he is really scary,
You never know, he might be hairy,
He could be fat,
He might even be a bat,
You will scream,
He will catch you
By the stream,

Run, run, as fast as you can,
He is right behind you,
He has a really sharp fang,
You run too fast for him
His name is Grim,
Good, he is dead,
Now I can go to my bed.

Jade Reeveley (9)
Mill O' Forest Primary School, Stonehaven

In The Dark

In my bedroom in the night
I got such a fright
With the creaking and the squeaking floorboards.

They always make my dog bark as loud as he can
And sometimes I feel like cooking him
In a frying pan.

Heather Dryburgh (8)
Mill O' Forest Primary School, Stonehaven

Don't Go Near The Door

You don't go near the corner of the door
Because you don't know what's there
There may be a bat and it might give you a bite
In the middle of your old, messy flat.

There might be a sheep
But you want a peek
So you open the door and the gang of bats are there
Fluttering their black silky wings and giving you a fright
In the middle of the night.

Elliot Johnson (8)
Mill O' Forest Primary School, Stonehaven

War

Lots of detonation
There is evacuation
What is going to happen?
Are they going to live or die?
Bombs coming down
People are scared
Not knowing if they are coming back.

Hannah Mackenzie (10)
Mill O' Forest Primary School, Stonehaven

World War II

World War II was very scary
There was the sound of guns
But there were not a lot of buns
In World War II there were tears
And no cheers
And a lot of gas masks.

Jennifer Ogg (11)
Mill O' Forest Primary School, Stonehaven

The War

World War II,
To go back in time,
Would be my fear,
The German leader,
Adolf Hitler,
Caused lots of destruction,
Evacuations, gas masks, blackouts,
Air raid shelters and tears,
I'm glad I'm not in the middle of World War II!

Sophie Christie (11)
Mill O' Forest Primary School, Stonehaven

War!

War, war, such a terrible thing,
Lots of children evacuees,
Leaving behind their families,
I hate the air raids and living rough,
There were some survivors,
That's good enough!

Finlay Milne (11)
Mill O' Forest Primary School, Stonehaven

World War II

I don't like war,
It's a horrible thing,
Destruction, demolition, disaster,
Bombs, guns, explosives,
Tanks with their ranks,
When it stopped,
People cheered, but still
Not normal for a few years.

Emma Gordon (11)
Mill O' Forest Primary School, Stonehaven

War

War is horrific,
Makes me think of fear,
Death, destruction and danger,
The three Ds of war,
Survivors do emerge,
But there is a flipside -
War claims many lives.

Grant Begg (11)
Mill O' Forest Primary School, Stonehaven

War

War makes me think
About bombs, cruelty and death,
Missiles are fired,
People drop dead,
What a shock
Their families will get,
Sirens give warning
That bombs are here,
That's the war -
Fright and fear.

Becca Stewart (11)
Mill O' Forest Primary School, Stonehaven

War!

In war it is scary,
With all the bombs and fear,
All the people are taken by surprise,
Tanks!
Guns!
People!
Causing death.

Sarah-Louise Milne (11)
Mill O' Forest Primary School, Stonehaven

War

War has begun
Bombs and gasses
Germany, Britain and France
Going at it
Going into shelters
Blackouts everywhere
Planes and missiles
Prisoners going to Nazi prison camps
What a disaster!

Craig Forbes (11)
Mill O' Forest Primary School, Stonehaven

War

I hate the thought of war,
Bombs destroying houses,
Deaths and blackouts,
Planes, shelters and evacuees,
It's such an awful thought!
I hope it never comes again.

Hannah Duncan (10)
Mill O' Forest Primary School, Stonehaven

World War II

War has started, the fight has begun,
Homes have been hit and houses have been bombed,
People are angry, frightened and scared,
Children are taken to the countryside,
For the war has not ended,
It has just begun
And neither side has lost or won.

Rachel Eastcroft (11)
Mill O' Forest Primary School, Stonehaven

WWII

Would it be a good idea
If there was no war each year?
Would it be a good idea
If you couldn't make gas bombs appear?
Would it be a good idea
If we all had to be friends?

Ryan Brown (10)
Mill O' Forest Primary School, Stonehaven

Skater

There once was an ice-skater
That worked as a waiter
He knew he was good
But he ate dog food
So he won't go skating later!

Kerry Campbell (10)
Mill O' Forest Primary School, Stonehaven

Happiness

Happiness is yellow like the yellow sun
It tastes like vanilla ice cream
It smells like new spring flowers
It looks like baby lambs leaping
It sounds like fairies singing
It feels like a soft, playful kitten.

Karris Knowles (10)
Mill O' Forest Primary School, Stonehaven

Colours

What is yellow?
Yellow is the moon shining in the night
Yellow is the sun shining bright
Yellow is the stars up high
Yellow is a bee buzzing about

What is red?
Red is poppies thinking of the people who died
Red is a rose all on its own
Red is blood from someone getting hurt
Red is the colour of love on Valentine's Day

What is green?
Green is Mill O' Forest winning the green flag
Green is trees in summer but not in winter
Green is land, blue is sea
Green is plants that help us breathe.

Fiona Craigen (10)
Mill O' Forest Primary School, Stonehaven

The Sun

The sun is so hot
The sun is so small
From a distance
It looks like a ball.

Douglas Blacklaw (10)
Mill O' Forest Primary School, Stonehaven

The Universe

Shiny,
Glistening, stars,
Floating, sparkly, spaceships,
Eclipses happening every so often,
Darkness.

Megan McMillan (10)
Mill O' Forest Primary School, Stonehaven

Spring!

S ome new flowers blossom
P rimroses and
R ed roses
I love spring with all the newborn animals
N ow I like spring, but here comes summer
G reen is the grass that the animals eat.

India Henderson (9)
Mill O' Forest Primary School, Stonehaven

Dancing

Dancing,
Active, enjoyable,
Swirling, jumping, sliding,
Fun, interactive, competitive,
Singing.

Lucia Arandia (10)
Mill O' Forest Primary School, Stonehaven

Fear

Fear is black and grey
It tastes like cold sausages
It smells like hate
It looks like a stormy night
It sounds like someone following you
If feels like someone watching you!

Jordan Henderson (10)
Mill O' Forest Primary School, Stonehaven

Skating

I love skating in my free time
Put on my skates . . . gloves . . . scarf
Time to skate all day long.

When I come off the rink . . .

Take my skates off . . . gloves off . . . scarf off
Put the gloves and scarf in my bag
Put the skates back
Heading back in the car
Happy!

Jordan Butchart (10)
Mill O' Forest Primary School, Stonehaven

The Writer Of This Poem
(Based on 'The Writer of this Poem' by Roger McGough)

The writer of this poem
Is helpful to my teacher
As tidy as my bedroom
As fast as Gavin Henson
As kind as charity.

As cute as a bunny
As thirsty as a plant
As fat as a plum
As thoughtful as my dad.

As cool as a cat
As nice as my sister
As greedy as a crocodile
As wicked as a witch.

The writer of this poem
Is as cool as can be
She's as beautiful as a rose
And of course, that is me!

Cerys James (7)
Nant Y Parc Primary School, Senghenydd

The Writer Of This Poem
(Based on 'The Writer of this Poem' by Roger McGough)

As kind as my mammy
As cute as a puppy
As funny as my daddy
As charming as a princess
As tidy as my room
As small as an ant
As thirsty as a camel
As hungry as a kitten

As artistic as my friend
As cheeky as a monkey
As cuddly as my teddy bear
As pretty as a peacock

The writer of this poem
Is cute and as funny as can be
She's a delight to know
And of course, that's me!

Ella Day (7)
Nant Y Parc Primary School, Senghenydd

The Writer Of This Poem
(Based on 'The Writer of this Poem' by Roger McGough)

The writer of this poem
Is as loud as a wolf
As playful as a puppy
As cute as a kitten
As pretty as a peach
As shy as an antelope
As slow as a tortoise
As wise as an owl
As nice as a watermelon
As kind as a nurse
As helpful as can be
As polite as you can get

The writer of this poem
Is as cool as she can be
She's thoughtful, polite and clever
And of course, that is me!

Sophie Birkinshaw (7)
Nant Y Parc Primary School, Senghenydd

The Writer Of This Poem
(Based on 'The Writer of this Poem' by Roger McGough)

The writer of this poem
Is as loud as can be
As shy as a mouse
As friendly as a cat
As tidy as my mum

As chatty as can be
As kind as my mum
As tall as a giraffe
As happy as a lark

As playful as a puppy
As fast as Wayne Rooney
As brainy as an owl
As cute as a kitten

The writer of this poem
Is as cool as can be
And of course, that is me!

Nadine Thomas (8)
Nant Y Parc Primary School, Senghenydd

The Writer Of This Poem
(Based on 'The Writer of this Poem' by Roger McGough)

Is very good
As fast as David Beckham
As quiet as a mouse
As brainy as an owl

As big as an elephant
As good as gold
As thoughtful as my mother
As mad as my brother

As cool as a hedgehog
As kind as my mother
As hard as metal
As healthy as my dad

The writer of this poem
Is as cool as can be
Clever, quiet and thoughtful
And of course, that is me!

Izaak Wallen (7)
Nant Y Parc Primary School, Senghenydd

The Writer Of This Poem
(Based on 'The Writer of this Poem' by Roger McGough)

Is as brainy as an owl
As fast as Wayne Rooney
As big as a twig
As friendly as can be

As happy as a lark
As small as an ant
As playful as a puppy
As cute as a kitten

As loud as a drum
As fat as a mat
As kind as my mother
As greedy as a monkey

The writer of this poem
Is as good as he can be
He's as cool as a pool
And of course, that is me!

Lewis Thomas (7)
Nant Y Parc Primary School, Senghenydd

The Writer Of This Poem
(Based on 'The Writer of this Poem' by Roger McGough)

The writer of this poem
Is as friendly as can be
As chatty as a chatterbox
As loud as a foghorn
As playful as a puppy

As kind as my mother
As tall as a giraffe
As brainy as an owl
As fast as Wayne Rooney

As cute as a kitten
As lazy as a lion
As strong as my dad
As scary as a ghost

The writer of this poem
Is as loud as can be
He's as good as gold
And of course, that is me!

James Ritchings (7)
Nant Y Parc Primary School, Senghenydd

When I Grow Up

When I grow up
I want to be just like my brother
A RAF Wing Commander
He flies jets over Iraq.
He shoots bombs over enemy lines
He saves his mates' lives.
I want this dream to come true.

Gethin Pearce (9)
Nant Y Parc Primary School, Senghenydd

When I Grow Up

When I grow up, I would like to be a fireman
My grandfather was a fireman
If we did not have them, we would be burnt to death
They are always sliding down shiny poles

When I grow up, I would like to be a policeman
My brother is a policeman
They save people from robbers

When I grow up, I would like to be a paramedic
My father is a paramedic
If we did not have them
Everybody would die from being ill

When I grow up, I would like to be a gardener
My auntie is a gardener
If we did not have them
Everything would not be pleasant.

Tim Crothers (9)
Nant Y Parc Primary School, Senghenydd

I'm Glad We Have

I'm glad we have mothers
They look after us when we are sick.
I'm glad we have policemen
Otherwise there'd be riots everywhere.
I'm glad we have firemen
They save our lives.
I'm glad we have grandparents
Because they look after us.
I'm glad we have families
Because they are nice.
All of them are nice
And they look after you.

Aliesha Crowley
Nant Y Parc Primary School, Senghenydd

When I Grow Up

When I grow up . . .
I am going to be a fireman
Because they get cats down from trees
And they put out fires.

When I grow up . . .
I am going to be a doctor
Because they give you X-rays
Medicine and tablets.

If we didn't have a bus driver . . .
We would have to walk to the . . .
Park, school, police station, fire station, ambulance station.

I am glad we have . . .
Trees, because the trees give us oxygen
Water and paper.

Jack Cossins (9)
Nant Y Parc Primary School, Senghenydd

My Messy Bedroom

A wardrobe with a broken door
Toys lying on the floor
I've got a carpet that is green
Some things are lost and can't be seen
Me playing on the Nintendo 64
'Danger Daniel!' on my bedroom floor
A window with a frame that's white
Through it the garden is in sight
A Game Boy that is small and red
My great, blue, messy bunk bed.

Daniel Banister (10)
Pittencrieff Primary School, Dunfermline

My Garden

Mossy pond with disgusting water, with a border of lilies
Busy bees with mellow yellow fur
The lavender smells really sweet on a summer's day
Rustling leaves in the trees in a relaxed atmosphere
Soft rose petals up the side of the lawn, coloured rosy red
The sun sets on the floral greenhouse
Every night with a shimmery tint.

Shaun Cuthbert (10)
Pittencrieff Primary School, Dunfermline

In My Snow Garden

In my garden I can feel a cool breeze
I smell the scent of fir trees that are rustling in the wind
I feel calm
I can feel the frost of snowflakes melting on my nose
I can hear the robins singing a very lovely Christmas tune
I can see my pond is frozen and is sparkling in the light
I feel energetic so I build a snowman
With coal eyes and smile and a carrot for the nose
I can hear distant laughter and the traffic up the road
I wish that all this would last forever.

Marie Sarah Philbin (10)
Pittencrieff Primary School, Dunfermline

My Hamster, Sam

My hamster, Sam, is light brown,
He will always cheer you up when you're down.
Even if he bites your finger,
You'll just have to linger!
He has a cute furry face,
You could try and have a race.
He loves to play in his ball,
He's not a bad hamster at all!
When he runs his tail is wagging about,
He has a cute little snout,
You should see him!

Jenny Milne (10)
Pittencrieff Primary School, Dunfermline

Autumn

Hear fluttering leaves falling from an old oak tree
Smell damp leaves
See the bare, brown, ugly trees
All the leaves lying lonely
Feel the cool breeze on your cold cheek
Hear children jumping happily in the damp, crunchy leaves
All the mellow yellow and rosy red leaves lying on the ground
Hear conkers falling to the ground
Making big plopping noises when they fall.

Mairi Munro (10)
Pittencrieff Primary School, Dunfermline

The Garden

Lying in the long green grass, calm and relaxed
Wood pigeons in the trees, singing with the birds
Mellow yellow-coloured sunflowers standing in bright sun
The rich, sweet, heavy smell of lavender in the gentle breeze
Listening to the tranquil pond, with the splashing frogs
The rustling leaves in the old oak trees, by the cool breeze
Rosy red roses with their soft, velvety petals
The garden shines and sparkles in the summer sun.

Matthew Koch (10)
Pittencrieff Primary School, Dunfermline

I Love My Rabbit

I have a rabbit called Flopsy
She loves to bounce
She loves to pounce
She lives in a hutch
Of her we think much.
She loves to hop
She loves to play
And she will hop every day.
She has a cute furry face
And would like to have a race.
When she's in the run
She has so much fun.

Michael Waterworth (10)
Pittencrieff Primary School, Dunfermline

Snowy Winter

In winter, glistening snow falls from gutters
Sledges skid and swerve around old, snowy gardens
The sound of children's laughter
Waking up everyone in the street
Children throw snowballs
Flying everywhere, hitting cars and windows
Sparkling snowflakes
Touch the ground like feathers
Icy cold snow
Freezing cars and people
Cars driving their engines as hard as they can
They are stuck in the snow.

Ross Atherton (9)
Pittencrieff Primary School, Dunfermline

World War II

People armed head to toe with machine guns
And are fitted with camouflaged suits.
You hear whistling gun bullets
Piercing the air like a jet plane.
You feel as if you are in an alley of destruction.
The pungent powder of guns
Choking smoke from burning houses
Stings your eyes like mad.
Houses are frying
While people are dying
The injured are lying
And children are crying.

Mark Avery (9)
Pittencrieff Primary School, Dunfermline

My Summer Poem

Children laughing in the sun
Shouting at everyone there
Melting chocolate on a little boy's hand
Delicate flowers are sitting in the sand
I hear lots of dogs barking and cars parking
Everyone's face looks like fiery red!
Kids are throwing beach balls into the salty, calm sea!
Mums and dads are sunbathing
Lifeguards are kept busy
Old men and women are spying
Little children and babies are crying
In the flaming orange sun!

Afton Ritchie (9)
Pittencrieff Primary School, Dunfermline

Walking In Autumn

Walking through the wood in autumn
Listening to the sound of leaves crunching under your feet
With the smell of autumn in the air
Seeing bare trees with no leaves
Colours of hot orange and fire-red
Cool breeze picking up the leaves on the ground
Making the leaves run
Walking on to see many more sensational things.

Bethoch McLeman (10)
Pittencrieff Primary School, Dunfermline

Me In My Garden

Doing cartwheels in the long, moist, green grass
I feel so energetic among all the colours
Of the mellow yellow sunflowers that seem to scrape the clouds
The shimmering greens reflect on the sparkling water in the pond
The blood-red roses and the pearly-pink roses
Standing next to a neat row of peachy-tinted tulips.

Sitting on the creamy-painted bench to regain my breath
A slight, warm breeze carries the scent
Of a rich, sweet lavender fragrance
Freshly cut grass and new-bedded hay from the guinea pig's hutch.

I swing from a thick branch on the strong, towering rowan tree
I stop to listen to the humming of a pair of busy bees
The twittering of the hedge sparrows from the neighbour's hedge wall
The faint splashes of frogs in the pond.

That's me in my garden
And what makes me feel free.

Rhea Patel-McCrossan (10)
Pittencrieff Primary School, Dunfermline

In The Garden

Time to go outside to play
I wonder what we will see today
In the old oak tree
Two owls and babies, three
Busy, buzzy bees
Flying in the trees
In tall green grass
I really feel relaxed
When there is a breeze
I am as frisky as a flea
I can run around the garden
Energetically, *wheeee!*
Sitting beside the pond shimmering so blue
I will get a drink for me and for you
Singing birds, crows and all
I wonder if they fly away at fall
It's getting dark now
Time to go.

Paige Summerson (9)
Pittencrieff Primary School, Dunfermline

Guess Who?

The brown wooden door loomed closer,
My white trembling hand reached out to the door handle,
It creaked open, slowly,
A strong scent of powder drifted out of the room,
In it, there were brown teddies on a shelf,
In the corner was a white cot,
A blue cotton blanket lay in the cot,
A little pink head was sticking out,
It moved about and its head was as soft as a rose's petals.

It is my little brother, Finn!

Jade McCathie (10)
Pittencrieff Primary School, Dunfermline

Dinosaurs

Calm water rushing by with the swishing trees
The ground rumbling as the dinosaurs thunder by
A stegosaurus and a megasaurus lumber by
The iguanodon eggs in their nest, impatiently waiting for their mum
T-rex lumbers to the water for a massive drink
Stegosaurus fights with a tyrannosaurus rex
But the tyrannosaurus rex wins.

Morgan Steedman (10)
Pittencrieff Primary School, Dunfermline

The Garden

I see mellow yellow sunflowers
I feel a small breeze rushing through my very soul
I can hear wasps and bees passing by my ears
I can hear and see the splashing, sparkling, blue pond
I feel happy
I see rosy-red tulips and beautiful roses.

Daniel Halpin (10)
Pittencrieff Primary School, Dunfermline

The Beach

Lying on soft sand
Feeling relaxed
Watching the sea splashing up
And down
Listening to the children
Laughing, feeling joyful
Feeling the cold ice cream melting
Sticky on your hand
Sun sparkling on the shimmering
Blue sea
Listening to the busy buzzy
Bees buzzing around
Watching the birds flying
Round and round in the
Sky
Smelling the hot, steamy food
In the café.

Eve Mossman (9)
Pittencrieff Primary School, Dunfermline

Winter

Snow falling from the sky
Dogs and children playing in the snow
Children falling into the snow
Playing snow fights
Christmas bells ring every morning
Christmas lights glowing from people's homes
People giving Christmas cards
At the hot, red, fire
Children are sleeping
This is winter.

Dina Campbell (9)
Pittencrieff Primary School, Dunfermline

The Dragon!

By the village, there's a cave,
Dark, cold and damp,
Where the dragon lives,
He is fast,
He is old,
He is smart,
He is fearless,
He is going to have us for dinner.

So watch out village,
If you're asleep, be on your guard,
Or he might come and get you,
If you run, he will find you,
So run and hide, run, run, run!

He will get you if you don't
Don't listen to his
Terrifying

Roar!
Or you will go *deaf!*

Karl McClean (10)
Victoria Primary School, Carrickfergus

Lion Hunter!

In the jungle, trudging through trees and leaves,
Waiting, watching, camping . . .
Is the lion hunter and if he sees a lion
He will skulk around
And
When the lion least expects it . . . *boom!*
He attacks, fires, kills and smiles,
For not only does he have food,
He also has fur!

Later, he goes back and does exactly the same thing again,
Cutting through vines, trudging through elephant dung,
Spiders' eyes and an assortment of other nasty things.
Trudging, stopping, listening, shooting
And going on again, always watching, waiting, camping . . .
The lion hunter is no fool!

The end!
(At least for the lion, that is!)

David Robert Algeo Douglas (10)
Victoria Primary School, Carrickfergus

Noisy Things

A wailing siren coming from a speeding police car
Deafening guns heard during the dark and dangerous war
Banging drums along the streets on the 12th of July
The crashing sea against the rocks on a wild stormy day
A trumpeting elephant performing tricks in the circus
A crying baby waking the house in the middle of the night.

Shouting children running around the street at midnight
Spooky movies scaring the audience and waking the dead
Rumbling vacuum sucking up the dust in the hall
Crashing tools annoy everyone who is near
A breathtaking football match finishes with a draw and the crowd yell
Amazing fireworks make you stop and stare.

Courtney Gibb (9)
Victoria Primary School, Carrickfergus

That Smell

The smell that drifts through the room
The smell that is not yucky fumes
The smell that makes me want to say
Hurry up and make my day
That smell doesn't last
That smell is the past
That smell can't be mine
But that smell can be a sign.

The smell as you walk down the stairs
The smell that makes you pull your hairs
That smell has to be mine
But I hope it is not wine
Leave me be I have to say
Get my smell and then I'll play
Go off and leave me be
That smell is near me
That smell can hear me
If I go to the kitchen I bet it will be Dad cooking chicken
Oh dear, I was wrong, I found out that it was Mum
Please Mum, forgive me and then I'll let my smell go free.

Judith Louise Scott (9)
Victoria Primary School, Carrickfergus

My Little Black Rabbit

My little black rabbit
Has a funny bunny snout
And also did I tell you
She can count.

My little black rabbit
Plays with me all day
But when it comes to bedtime
She snuggles up in her hay.

My little black rabbit
Loves all the healthy stuff
If you were to eat it
You would become a ball of fluff.

My little black rabbit
Is the cutest rabbit you've ever seen
And if you don't say so
You are mean!

Jamie Lee Livingston (9)
Victoria Primary School, Carrickfergus

Noisy Things

Trickling waterfall running through the tropical forest
A roaring lion scaring everybody out of the zoo
Smashing hailstones hitting off the car window on an awful rainy day
Cheering football match being played on a warm afternoon
A blasting rocket shooting through the dark and starry night
A buzzing bee flying through the bright blue sky.

Nicola Jayne Curran (9)
Victoria Primary School, Carrickfergus

The Lioness

The lioness roars madly,
She sneaks up behind you, camouflaged,
Though she looks cute,
She likes chewing on my boot.

She used to live in a den,
Just until she turned ten,
She plays with her brothers and sisters
And sometimes gets thorns and blisters.

Now she is sick,
Oh, please don't die,
Just once more,
The lioness roars madly.

Danielle Lesley Brush (9)
Victoria Primary School, Carrickfergus

Noisy Things

A wailing siren coming from a speeding police car
Deafening guns heard during the dark and dangerous war
Banging drums along the streets on the 12th of July
The crashing sea against the rocks on a wild, stormy day
A trumpeting elephant performing tricks at the circus
A crying baby waking the house in the middle of the night
The bashing fireworks flashing in the middle of Oxford Street
The yelling teenagers on the ride in Carrick fair
The thumping speakers were playing all night in my sister's room
The rowdy crowds at the football match, cheering for Man U
The splashing rain was really bad on a windy night
The hammering tools in my grandad's noisy shed.

Naomi Hannah Watson (10)
Victoria Primary School, Carrickfergus

Hallowe'en

Hallowe'en is a fright
The ghosts' and witches' favourite night
A really scary, spooky sight

Fireworks lighting up the sky
Having a slice of hot apple pie
Pumpkins looking with their evil eye

Trick or treat for a bag of sweets
Making costumes out of sheets
Little ghosts filling the streets.

Rory Aron Magill (9)
Victoria Primary School, Carrickfergus

Animal Madness

Some animals have paws
And some have claws,
All different shapes and sizes.

Leopards are spotty
And tigers are stripy
And lots of different colours.

I love cute cats
But I'm afraid
Of scary bats.

I'm mad about dogs
And my nana has frogs
In her lovely garden.

There are fish in reefs
And seals in the sea,
We are all animals, you and me.

Foxes and ox,
Camels and mammals,
So I guess all I'm trying to say
Is I am mad about *animals!*

Ellen Crawford (9)
Victoria Primary School, Carrickfergus

Animals

Animals come in different sizes and shapes
From a small, little mouse
To a big, giant ape
Some fly in the sky
Some swim in the sea
Some live down a hole
Or up in a tree
My favourite animal lives in a stable
He sleeps on hay and not on a table
It eats apples and carrots
And straw and oats
And to keep warm in winter
It grows a thick coat
Can you guess what it is?
It's a horse, of course!

Rebekah Kirkpatrick (9)
Victoria Primary School, Carrickfergus

Animals

There are so many animals in the world,
There's the crocodile, shark and even the bird,
There are ostriches, parrots and even reindeer,
My goodness, so many great animals here.

There's also the lion, he's the king of the jungle,
If you torment him, he'll give you a tumble,
There's the lioness too, she's as quick as lightning,
If you torment her, she'll be very frightening.

We mustn't forget the cats and the dogs,
Hamsters and guinea pigs, snakes and frogs,
We should love all animals and be good to them too,
For they are all God's creatures, just like me and you.

Matthew Hogg (9)
Victoria Primary School, Carrickfergus

Wet, Wet, Wet Day

Rain, rain pouring down outside
What shall we do?

We can't go out
And play on the swings

Oh, I wish the rain would stop
So we can go and play

The rain has stopped
The rain has stopped
Now we can go out and play

I'm going to play with my friends,
Oh no, the rain is on again.

Rebecca Anderson (10)
Victoria Primary School, Carrickfergus

I Am A Baby Elephant

I am a baby elephant, cute and friendly
I am the colour peach, warm and kind
I am a tasty burger, scrumptious and mouthwatering.

I am a rose, fresh and happy
I am a book, full of words and information
I am a white cloud, soft and fluffy
I am a bar of chocolate, sweet and yummy.

Gemma McArthur (9)
Victoria Primary School, Carrickfergus

Me, Me, Me, All About Me!

I am a feisty tiger, fun too, of course
I am a red tomato, blazing warm
I am a chocolate apple, cool and appetising
I am a hanging-out T-shirt, lazy and brilliant
I am a wonderful make-up artist, cool and the best
I am a dictionary, full of words to say to people
I am a sunflower, big and bright
I am a wonderful person, but big and bold
I am a thunderstorm, mad and anxious.

Erin McKeown (10)
Victoria Primary School, Carrickfergus

I Am A Berserk Gorilla

I am a berserk gorilla, never sitting still
I am the colour silver, stronger than a metal pole
I am a computer, with lots of information
I am an orange, with lots of pieces to my life
I am a deadly hurricane, rampaging away
I am a joke book, with lots of jokes inside
I am a swarm of locusts, eating everything in my way.

Jason Kennedy (10)
Victoria Primary School, Carrickfergus

The Crazy Duck

I am a crazy duck, quaky and snappy
I am the colour blue, cold and relaxed
I am as good as gold, my mum says, but I am not really
I am as cool as a computer, funny and smart
I am fit and playful
I am a storm, fast and noisy
I am fierce like a tiger, rough and tough
I am a quilt, lovely and cosy.

Marc William Templeton (9)
Victoria Primary School, Carrickfergus

I Am A Soft Duvet

I am a strong gorilla, rough and tough
I am a red chilli, hot and spicy
I am a pink rose, warm and fuzzy
I am a breezy green, cool and windy
I am a soft duvet, fluffy and cosy
I am an exciting book, magical and expressing
I am an expensive pair of jeans, trendy and beautiful.

Clara Eve Montgomery (9)
Victoria Primary School, Carrickfergus

I Am . . .

I am the colour green, mean and lean
I am a mole, short-sighted and small
I am a ruby, precious and shiny
I am a cobra, deadly and quick
I am a chilli pepper, hot and spicy
I am the sun, warm and bright
I am a brick, hard and strong.

Andy Wilson (9)
Victoria Primary School, Carrickfergus

I Am

I am a giraffe, tall and long
I am the colour blue, cool and calm
I am skinny chips in hot grease
I am a daisy, crazy and lazy
I am a pair of trousers, hip and pop
I am a fish, swimming in the sea
I am a teddy bear with big eyes and a black nose.

Rebecca McCausland (9)
Victoria Primary School, Carrickfergus

I Am . . .

I am lazy and huffy, like a cat
I am always chilly
I am as funny as a banana split
I am as pink as a rose
I am a little princess
I am a little angel
I am as good as gold
I am like the colour pink.

Shannon Laughlin (10)
Victoria Primary School, Carrickfergus

I Am A Tiny Cat, Mad And Bad

I am a tiny cat, mad and bad
I am heavy pumps, *rata-tap-tap*
I am a red rose, rosy and nosy
I am the colour pink, light and right
I am a daisy, crazy and lazy
I am a top, cool like school
I am a corn on the cob, buttery and fluttery.

Kennedy Herron (9)
Victoria Primary School, Carrickfergus

A Poem About Me!

I am an angry giant, tall and strong
I am black and white like a football
I am a magical book, colourful and long
I am a pair of scissors, sharp and pointy
I am an orange basketball, *bounce, bounce*
I am smart, like an elephant
I am like a fish, *splash, splash*
I am like the sun, so warm.

Matthew Larkham (9)
Victoria Primary School, Carrickfergus

My Poem

I am an angry lion, hard and rough
I am the colour gold, shiny and smooth
I am a rose
I am bright red
I am a coat, soft and long
I am a banana, very bendy.

Aimee Patterson (9)
Victoria Primary School, Carrickfergus

I Am A Cute Rabbit!

I am a cute rabbit, bouncing around
I am a pair of jeans, hip and trendy
I am a cheeky monkey, messy and fun
I am a sweet rose, long and sweet
I am a pair of pumps, always dancing around
I am the colour blue, calm and happy.

Chloe Park (9)
Victoria Primary School, Carrickfergus

I Am A Little Monkey

I am a little monkey, cheeky and mean
I am the colour red, bright and rosy
I am a broken Hoover, cannot clean up
I am a lazy cat, tired and sleepy
I am a gentle wind, fresh and breezy
I am a teddy bear, cuddly and friendly
I am a bouncy ball, bouncing with fun
But most of all, I am me
And that's how it should be!

Katherine McKinley (10)
Victoria Primary School, Carrickfergus

All About Me

I am a bulldog, rough and tough
I am a deadly hawk, quick and unseen
I am the colour black, smart and dark
I am a tasty pizza, nice and sweet
I am a sunny day, bright and cheerful
I am a toy, fun and playful
I am a quiet cat, fast and silent.

Paul Nelson (10)
Victoria Primary School, Carrickfergus

Angry Boy, Tough And Rough

I am an angry boy, tough and rough
I am a lazy brother, playing the PlayStation
I am a bulldog, fierce and hungry
I am the colour red, as fast as lightning
I am a football, hitting the back of the net
I am a footballer, scoring goals
I am dangerous thunder, scary and dark.

Jordan McCully (10)
Victoria Primary School, Carrickfergus

Unique Things About Me

I am an elephant, strong and lean
I am lightning, quick and mean
You should see me play for the team!
I am a book, like 'The Famous Five'
I am adventurous and I am wild
I am a chilli, sweet and spicy
I am a pink T-shirt, light and bright
I am a screaming police car, ear-splitting and fast.

Katie Ann Houston (9)
Victoria Primary School, Carrickfergus

I Am Cool Lightning

I am an angry lion, deadly hungry
I am the colour blue, cool and relaxed
I am stylish, baggy jeans, trendy and handsome
I am a daisy, waving in the rain
I am a sofa, lounging in the sun
I am a cool place
I am noisy lightning, slick and fast.

Joshua Daly (9)
Victoria Primary School, Carrickfergus

I Am A Cheeky Monkey

I am a cheeky monkey, crazy and fun
I am a pretty pink rose, sweet and cute
I am a baggy pair of jeans, calm and cool
I am a lovely rainbow, neat and stylish
I am a tropical drink, delicious and fruity
I am a hockey stick, thin and playful
I am a little clarinet, musical and happy.

Cara Leathem (9)
Victoria Primary School, Carrickfergus

I Am Me

I am a dark blue, mysterious and slick
I am a camouflaged leopard, I never stop moving
I am an eyeball, I like to watch stuff
I am the sky, high with thoughts
I am a cool tree, tall and stylish
I am a cheeky monkey, clever and messy.

Alex Steenson (9)
Victoria Primary School, Carrickfergus

Every Single Night

When I go up the stairs at night,
It gives me such a terrible fright.
Floorboards creaking,
Voices speaking,
Every single night.

The scary monsters under my bed,
The fluffy pillow over my head.
I hear some feet,
Oh, I can't sleep!
Every single night.

I hear the feet getting closer,
The eyes move on my poster.
I start to suck my thumb,
But who comes in the door, but Mum!
Every single night.

Mum comes in, switches on the light,
And she says, 'Did I give you a fright?'
Mum goes out and a voice says . . .
'Sleep tight, have a dreadful night!'

Lucy Hannah Sempey (9)
Victoria Primary School, Carrickfergus